Sexuality and Sadism

Sexuality and Sadism

Mbangu Mangala
wa MANGALA wa KABASUKUPA ne MATANDU wa BUANA

EDITION : BABA MATANDU NE NGALULA

This book was printed in the United States of America.

To order additional copies of this book, contact:
Xlibris Corporation
1-888-795-4274
www.Xlibris.com
Orders@Xlibris.com
58183

TABLE OF CONTENTS

TO My WIFE TSHITUKA MBANGU
To My Family
And to My Family-in-law

ABSTRACT

This paper explores the difference between sexuality and sexual sadism. Many people tend to confuse sexuality and sexual sadism; the latter is not socially acceptable. However, the enactment of sexual sadism can be facilitated by culture, which avoids confronting issues related to sexuality.

Talking clearly about sex is often forbidden by many cultures, which is why people use symbols and figures of speech to talk about sexuality.

The methodology included literature review and a questionnaire. Some French articles were translated to English by the author of this paper. During the interviews subjects were open about their ideas and their feelings.

The findings of this paper support the view that sex education is enacted and more candors about sex in society and in the home leads to healthy sexual behaviors between couples.

CHAPTER 1

Introduction

The goal of this study is to sensitize experts to their educational role for society. Experts need to continue their role of educators to society. They cannot for one reason or another, become complacent and abdicate their role. Their knowledge to help those who live in confusion or those who lack knowledge. This topic is of importance because it turns out that many people have confusion when they try to describe sexual practices and behaviors. Even educated people have the same confusion. A case in point was one of my friends who, because of lack of knowledge, confused sexual sadism with sexuality that was normal.

Everyone in many ways knows sexuality. Many times, friends, comrades, pals are like teachers and advisers. They can talk among themselves without inhibition and say things they have heard about or practiced somewhere. Often, there can be confusion between sexuality and sadism. This is dangerous because sexuality is not sadism, and people should not practice sadism as an excuse that this is general normal sexuality. To learn more about this confusion, I had discussions with people who are tolerant of sexual sadism. Tolerance should not facilitate a social phenomenon like sadism to expand. An example of tolerance is when societies have, in the past, tolerated bestiality. In modern times this is regarded as a perversion. Tolerance of bestiality, sadism, and other forms of sexual perversion do not promote healthy development in society. This paper will attempt to address these issues.

With regard to sadism this paper will explore sexuality and the roles of fantasy. The methodology relies on a literature review, a questionnaire, interviews and a discussion of the findings. The findings reveal that people can usually define sexuality, even if it is with difficulty, and that they do not accept sadism, which is regarded as deviant and perverse.

Good manner: (Working Mother, February/March 2009.)

Sexuality is subject to cultural influences. Some people in modern countries think that this is not the case. People often try to experiment but even this is influenced by culture. Many people believe sexuality is a gift from God. This is a more traditional and religious point of view. In the modern world sex has also became a business. One can cite websites, pornography, prostitution, sexually explicit media and music, where sex is used and sold as merchandise.

Sexuality and sex are also used in politics and public relations. Nations have been united because of the marriage between princes, kings, and ambassadors. Many agreements have been made via marriage and / or sexual liaisons. Sometimes harmony between companies, governments and nations is guaranteed by the existence of sexual relations between key people in positions of power.

Sexuality is important to humans; because our very existence is as a direct result of sexual relations between two people we also often feel we must respect and take care of sexuality and sexual issues. Sexuality is life; nobody could exist without being impacted by it. Many believe that we continue God's work of creation by expressing sexuality.

This paper posits that it is important that experts and specialists have a clear stance regarding normative sexuality. They must be able to advise people on these issues; often clients may be in a position to access this information. Often mental health specialists are called upon to help sort out accurate information from hearsay and superstition. They often must address difficult situations that survive on misinformation.

Many couples may come for counseling seeking information and support in managing their intimate couples' relationship, including their affective relations (such as their feeling of love for their partner) and their physical relationship. At the other end of the spectrum are those who seek, and who need help with their involvement in sexual perversions. An example mentioned earlier was bestiality. Sometimes people participate in this type of perversion because they are shy or have an aversion to human contact. These are not necessarily isolated cases; there are instances of animals being trained or conditioned to follow their trainer's will. These animals are offered for those interested in such perversions.

Usually people like to have sexual relations between persons of the opposite sex. Some like to have sex with a person of the same sex. Many religions prohibit having sex with the same sex partner. Yet people break the laws of religion or cultures to have forbidden relations. One can find this type of behavior in many human groups. Sexuality is a powerful force in human beings; when desire and attraction occur humans give in; sexual pleasure is a powerful motivation.

Some people inflict pain on the partner during sexual relations; these people are known as sadists. When this occurs between consenting adults one imposes the sadism on the partner who accepts it; this partner is the masochist. Generally the sadist feels pleasure by inflicting pain on the partner; the masochist feels pleasure by suffering. In most societies people have varying degrees of openness about normal sexuality. However acceptance of masochism is rare in societies as whole. Lots of people do not like to talk about sadism or masochism or other types of perversions.

Two issues need emphasis here. One is that perversions between non-consenting adults are not being examined in this paper. These include the infliction of pain on someone who doesn't consent; this is sexual abuse, which becomes a matter for the courts to judge. In every society many people are arrested and jailed because of it. Among the cases are also those of the sexual abuse of children. Among those jailed for this there can be even the parents.

The second point is that this author views homosexuality as a form of perversion despite the fact that this is not the prevalent scientific and medical view in this society. In the author's culture of origin, and for him personally, this is his position. While the values of this culture differ from that of the author he celebrates as normative the idea of heterosexuality:

"Love is magical and it can last if we remember differences". *(John, 1992, pp. 14).*

Good manner. (Ibid. Februaury/March 2009)

In many cultures same sex partners are viewed as a perversion because homosexuals and lesbians are believed to act by moral corruption; it is believed that they do not find an opposite sex partner, because they are shy or ashamed, because they are not able to convince the opposite sex partner, because it is easy to have many contacts with the same sex. Traditional societies believe that a perversion like this can start and then become a habit. Little by little they can have some others partners and the group continues; it can became big. Homosexuality is found many times in professional groups (churches, army). A lot of times it is also in mystic and spiritual groups which may have an objective to attain. Some groups may also recruit members. A lot of homosexuals may join these groups knowing why they are there; some become homosexuals due to ignorance of their true sexuality. In some groups money plays a great role for the first homosexual contact. This can also happen with heterosexual groups. Whenever sex is taboo it can make use of money or blackmail.

In any discussion of sex and sadism it is important to note the risks inherent. The clear example is HIV and AIDS. Sometimes when you ask a person with AIDS "how did you get that?" they may respond that they do not know. Some may try to remember recent sexual relations that occurred without precautions. In many societies a carrier of HIV is able to continue to transmit the disease to others. They do not think about the catastrophe they are spreading. It is the same for many perversions in the world. The perpetrators do not care about the catastrophe or social havoc they are creating.

Humans have been given many gifts and many ways to use them. But human beings also have perversions, which they are often at liberty to use. Culture becomes the guide for many.

CHAPTER 2

Definition and Discussion of Key Concepts

It is not easy to define sexuality because it is an affective and behavioral phenomenon. Many people experience their sexuality in different ways, which gives rise to many elastic definitions of sexuality. One can say sexuality is the condition characterized by sex. Sexuality demands the capacity to have sexual relations, or to engage in intercourse. It can also be a tendency toward excessive concern with sex. (Chaplin, 1985, pp. 422). Below are same key definitions:

Sadism is a sexual perversion in which sexual satisfaction is associated with the infliction of pain on the other. It is a psychological disorder in which sexual gratification is often solely derived from infliction of pain on others. (Ibid, pp. 406).

Dreams, images, fantasies, and sensory experiences have been defined in a variety of ways. Images and sensory awareness are one's connection to all of the possibilities that lie within. The most generally endorsed view is that the capacity for imagery is modified by learning and that learning never ends. Therefore the more one has a sexual relationship with someone, the more one-share experiences. This then leads to the acquisition of newer experiences.

In discussing Sigmund Freud, Richard S. Sharf (1999) states how:

> *Freud believed that human motivation was sexual in the broad sense that individuals were motivated to bring themselves pleasure. However, libido later came to be associated with all life instincts and included the general goal of seeking to gain pleasure and avoid pain. (Sharf, 1999, pp. 30).*

Human beings use sexuality for preservation. This process mitigates against loss, damage or neglect (Chaplin, 1985, pp. 422). Sexual pleasure is the result of sexual behavior. When two opposite sex partners engage in sexual acts they are seeking sexual pleasure, which leads to feelings of sexual wellbeing. That sexual wellbeing is the body's psychological and physical balance.

There are good and bad sexual relations; good sexual relations lead to happiness, the bad do not. But often partners do not show their feelings explicitly because sexual relations lead to the feigning of feeling; the partners may hide many feelings. Authors Scantling and Browder (1993) describe a case named Bret, 20 years old who states:

> *I didn't know what I was doing. It was all too new and I was so inexperienced. It was nervous. It was too quick, I didn't have time to get turned on or have an orgasm. Penetration was painful, and I didn't tell him. It felt too mechanical. I didn't know how I was supposed to feel. I felt it was wrong against everything I'd been taught. It's hard to relax when you feel that way! It was with a stranger, uncomfortable, no emotional attachment. I wasn't emotional ready, felt pressured and kind of used. I was raped the first time—it left emotional scars. (Scantling and Browder, 1993, pp. 16).*

Sadism is an adjacent action to sexuality. Sadism and Masochism derive from the kind of sexuality that inflicts pain on the victim; this behavior exists before, during or after sexual interaction. One interviewee described the following: before intercourse with his wife, he starts by slapping his wife until she cries and he sees the tears; once this occurs they have sexual intercourse. Sometimes his wife stays kneeling until she has pain and states she is in pain; once this occurs they have sex. If he forgets to let her kneel or forgets to slap her, she can not accept sexual interactions; she demands to be beaten before coupling. Union Review (1984) describes the case of M., (Union, November 1984, pp. 57) who is very happy because her husband treats her as a slave (Ibid, pp. 56). Another, P., has a fetish to submit to his wife when she is beating him (Ibid, pp. 58). Often sexual intercourse is performed without sadism; but sometimes sadism occurs before, during or after intercourse by certain sadists. Therefore sadism is not complimentary or necessary to perform a sexual act. Scantling and Browder state:

> *The road to supersex cannot be found by listening to external prescriptions. Achieving true sexual ecstasy involves not only listening*

to outside authorities, but mapping your own route to pleasure. They learned to trust their own inner guidance to lead them to what they need from the outside world (pp. 102). They know their own minds and are decisive and forceful enough to go after what they want. (Ibid, 1993, pp. 103).

In seeking pleasure humans use many ways; some of these ways are good, others are bad. The good are morally, psychologically and socially acceptable; the bad are not. The good ways lead to responsible sexuality, the accepting of responsibility to support sexuality and its consequences. The consequences range from relationships of friend, fiancée, wife, husband, and pregnancy and childrearing and on-going connections with off-spring. The bad ways lead to perversion and sadism, which include beating, whipping, slapping, sexual domination and bestiality. As mentioned earlier, in my view, they can also leads to homosexuality, which I personally regard as a perversion.

Consciousness: A human person is the only one to remember what happened before, during or after the sex act. He or she has awareness of the history of the sex act in which he or she engaged. One of the subjects of Scantling and Browder said:

Good manner. (Ibid. February/March 2009)

*I feel a sense of physical ecstasy, heat, and I tingle all over especially
my toes. Turning inside out of my body, merging with another or my
own mind, falling up, about to pass out, then release and relief. (
Ibid, 1993, pp. 26).*

About consciousness Dr Davidson said in the above text:

*The entire body surface is covered with potentially erogenous zones so
no stroke, touch, or nibble is inherently sexy. It is only when our minds
interpret a touch or feeling as sexy that we feel turned on. In short:
it is not just the body's physiological response, but the interaction of
the mind and the body that makes a sexual interlude disappointing
or joyous. (Ibid, pp. 24).*

Control: Many sexual experiences are planned; humans control the
steps: whom to meet? With whom to have sex? When? Before, during and
after intercourse the control comes from the sense of responsibility. Like
Scantling and Browder said:

*But isn't this a paradox-that to become supersexual, you must take control
of your life right up to the point where you must let go? Not at all. It
might help to think of controlling and letting go not as opposites, but as
complements, as parts of the same continuum. (Ibid, 1993, pp. 119).*

Sense of Oneness, of Unity and of Consciousness: Only human beings
can remember the experience before, during and after intercourse.
Psychologist Eric Fromm as quoted in Scantling and Browder wrote:

*The human desire to experience union with others is one of the strongest
motivators of human behavior . . . (We) human beings have lost our
original oneness with nature. In order not to feel utterly isolated-which
would, in fact, condemn us to insanity, we need to find a new unity:
with our fellow beings and with nature. (Ibid, 1993, pp. 49).*

Geri, a 46 years old physician, described by Sue and Sandra refers to this unity expressed during sex:

We're just so connected. When I'm touching him, I can almost sense what it feels like to be inside his skin being touched by me. (Ibid, 1993, pp. 49).

CHAPTER 3

Methodology

The methodology of this paper comprises two approaches: a literature review and an anonymous questionnaire administered as part of field research.

The texts that address sexual issues were in French; some others were in English. The French books were translated in English. In addition there was an anonymous questionnaire. Seven questions were administered to seven subjects who remain anonymous but who volunteered to do this. The answers were interpreted and are discussed in this paper.

The questions and the answers follow in this chapter. The subjects had the following professions: High school teachers (2), Administration (1), university teachers (2), and customers' representatives' (2).

The responses were given in the context of an appointment where they met with the interviewer for about three hours. The questionnaire was completed over a period of three days. The subjects were guaranteed anonymity.

CHAPTER 4

Literature Review

I read some reviews and discovered some information about sexuality and sadism. One source was the International Reviews section of Special Union, (May 1979), and Union # 149, (November 1984).

These reviews showed that there are two positions: sadist and masochist. The sadists inflict pain on others who accept it. People who accept the pain are the masochists. The sadists are gratified when they inflict pain on others and cause them to suffer. The masochists are gratified because they suffer. There are the provocative sadists and the provocative masochists. There are the consent sadist and the consent masochist. The provocatives initiate the situation; the consents accept the situation by sadistic role-playing. Below are the sadistic practices that were mentioned in these reviews.

One individual, Francisco, said in her letter:

I am very happy when I take sex with someone raping me; Many times I provoke and control all the situation until I am satisfied. Some times I take sex with a group of men like that. (Union, May 1979, pp. 48).

That is an example of a provocative masochist; the man or men are only the consent sadists playing a role. The true actor is Francisco.

Good manner. (Ibid. Februaury/March 2009)

Another case is from J.C. (Germany) who states: saying that:

He likes many times seeing or knowing that his wife is taking sex with someone else; she can tell him only the day and the moment; but it is not necessary for him to be there. The wife did it. (Ibid., pp. 140).

This is another case of a provocative masochist, he provokes the wife to have sex with someone else, and he is gratified by that. The wife accepts the sadist role by inflicting on her husband the pain he feels when she lets him know that she has another lover with whom she has sex. The husband is gratified when he is suffering.

JR talking about masochism said:

His partner (wife) asked him to put a chaste ring with a lock on his penis to prove his fidelity. The ring has to pass through the testicle purse to be locked together with the penis; doctors said: it is not a problem, but one thing is t take care of probable infection. (He was not clear at the end of his letter to let us know if he did it). (Union, May 1979. pp.143).

If Mr. JR did it he can be considered to be a consent masochist; if he did not do it he can be considered to be a non-consent masochist. In this case the wife is a provocative sadist. If the husband did it, she could be gratified as a provocative sadist; if he did not do it, she would not be gratified as a sadist, because the subject (husband) has not been a consent masochist.

P., (Toulon, France) describes his training for consent masochist, which happens little by little because his wife did not like to stop:

> *Evelyn, my spouse has many others lovers; she tried in the beginning to let me know that. I did not accept it, because it was painful for me in the beginning, but because my wife did not like to stop, I accepted the situation to satisfy her. She used to let me know the friends who have sex with her; when I am angry she says no, it is a game, and she does not love them, because it is a sexual joke, no love. (Union 149, November 1984, pp. 58).*

Bad manner by writing on the body. (Ibid. February/March 2009)

By saying what she is doing with others lovers, she is inflicting pain on her husband, who did not like to hear that in the beginning. But Evelyn liked to have sex with other lovers, and to tell her husband all her affairs with other lovers; she is looking only to inflict pain on her husband. She wants to be gratified through her husband's suffering. The more she talks about her lovers, the more husbands suffer. She is a provocative sadist; her husband was not a consent masochist, but then because he wanted to satisfy his wife, he became a consent masochist.

We read another case of a provocative masochist from Veronique who said;

I like to provoke my husband to beat me. When I am beaten, I asked to have sex with my husband to be calm, because after the taps I am very excited. I never complained about that; after sex having I am very happy. (Union # 149, November 1979, pp. 53).

This is a case of a provocative consent masochist. She likes to suffer and after suffering, she is gratified. The husband is a consent sadist role player. He received practice from his wife; he is now playing the sadist.

J.L. is a consent and provocative masochist. She stated:

I am twenty years old lady, I accept to have sex only after having been slapped; if my husband does not slap me, I refuse to have sex. Slapping is a sexual fetish for me; it is exciting for me. Intercourse after slapping is superb. (Union. # 149, November 1979, pp. 53).

This case is almost the same as the proceeding one; the wife is provocative and a consent masochist.

In these readings I learned that sexuality is power: it can push human beings to do things they would not normally do. Like Time Magazine described Monica Lewinsky and said:

A saga of an insecure and overweight child of a broken Beverly Hills home whose need for love and attention led her to seduce a President (March 15, 1999, pp. 30).

As the power of sexuality invades someone, he can not easily resist; many times, human beings are pushed to obey and to follow sadistic or masochist impulses.

Darla, one of Scatling and Browder subjects, described her sexual experiences:

I felt my body started to control me, and I did know what was happening. I did not feel ashamed or guilty. My mother did not tell me about sex, so I figured out, it was natural. My body felt strangely exciting. At first I just felt; but then it went on and on and on, and I let go. Suddenly I felt myself separated from my body. I felt, I was not in my body anymore. (1993, pp. 13).

In this case, an individual cannot control his behavior because he is urged by his sexual power; in this environment the sadist can gain gratification by inflicting pain on the consenting masochist. We know in these situation the lovers cry, yell, without knowing the sense or the meanings of their cries. They are following the feelings to do what they are impelled to do.

About her sadomasochism, Francisco said:

I am very happy when I take sex with someone who rapes me, many times I provoke someone who can play the sadistic role. I am going to control everything until I am satisfied. Some times I take sex with a group of men. Union Special, May 1979, pp. 48).

When she states that she is controlling every thing, it is not true, because she is acting under stimulation. The stimulant is the power to control the other's entire behavior. The body is overcome by the excitation. Catherine, 19, describes her excitation:

Suddenly, he walked here and there; it was this incredible electricity between us. We did not even say a word. He simply came over, lay down beside me, and we just took off! I instantly felt a sense of totally letting go, but not being afraid of losing control. I was like I was flying. (Scantling and Browder 1993, pp. 4).

CHAPTER 5

Field Research, Questionnaire and Findings.

people should not exaggerate; they indicated that this exaggeration means perversion or abuse such as we use some stimuli to alter the state of consciousness and behavior by drugs like alcohol, caffeine, nicotine for medicinal or non-medicinal proposes (Chaplin, 1985, pp. 139).

The fourth question was: Do you indulge in any sadistic practices?

Two people seemed to indicate that even if you like sadism, one should not do it; that means they felt it was The following is a list of the questions that were in the questionnaire administrated to subjects.

1. What does sexuality mean to you?
2. What does sadism mean to you?
3. Do you enjoy sexual interaction?
4. Do you indulge in any sadistic practices?
5. Do you believe laws can control sexuality?
6. Can laws control sadism and sadistic practices?
7. Would you like to add anything on the topic of sexuality and sadism?

The responses were in English as well as in French; the latter have been loosely translated into English by the author of this paper. The interviewees elaborated on their responses, which are discussed later.

We recollected the answers given by the persons during our testing. For the first question the following were the responses:

Love: (2); to have sex (2); loving (1); to live with opposite sex (1); to have baby (1).

For the second question the following were the responses:
Bad education (2); banditry (1); perversion (2); anomalous (1); anticultural (1).

For the third question the responses were:
yes (3); no exaggeration (2); that is live (1); to have baby (1).

For the fourth question the responses were: but not exaggeration (2); I let go but I do not do it (2); to please someone (1); it is love (1); why not (1).

For the fifth question the responses were:
no (2); not possible (2); the justice is not just (2); losing time (1).

For the sixth question the responses were:
I do not know it (1); Impossible (3); We do not talk about it (2); Some times (1).

For the seventh question the responses were:
Nothing (2); Sexuality is life (2); Sexuality must have a good education (2); Sexuality must be secret (1).

When at the end I would respond by thanking them, many people would end up laughing about *"thank you"*. When people are talking about sexuality, they look serious, but when they finish, they often start laughing. It is as if sexuality is a joke whose rules lie within each person but the answers are cultural. Each person knows that sexuality does not always conform to culture; it is a natural instinct but people encounter varied cultures in the expression of sexuality. They tried to convince the interviewer that they know what culture says about sex, and that they are somewhat conformist. People also felt some sense of embarrassment about being open about sex, especially when it had to do with sadism.

We administered 7 questions to seven people. Each question was answered in an elaborated discussion with the interviewer.

The first question was: what does sexuality mean to you?

Many answered that: sexuality is love (4); others said it is sex (3). These responses show that it is difficult for many people to give a precise answer about sexuality. People live out sexuality in their lives without knowing how to define explicitly what it really is. This difficulty is found to be common. In the media we observe be same difficulty.

Good manner. (Ibid. February/March 2009)

At the question is oral sex a sexual act? Monica Lewinsky responds:

> *This is hard for me to answer, in very . . . in a confined strict definition. In casual conversation, yes, it was. (Time Magazine, March 15, 1999, pp. 39).*

The journalist was confused too by calling sexuality sex. Sexuality can mean relations between two sexes; sex can refer to gender or to sexual intercourse. It is important to help people to avoid confusion between words and concepts, to be explicit about whether they mean contact between body parts that is sexually stimulating but may be distinguished from full sexual intercourse. It is also important to distinguish between anal, oral, vaginal intercourse and between masturbatory activity versus genital sexuality. Often people lack knowledge of precise terms and they use slang to describe these acts.

The second question was: What does sadism mean to you?

All the answers refereed to education. Lots of people responded that sadism is bad education (2); banditry (1); perversion (2); anomaly (1); anti culture (1). In short they describe sadism as a kind of bad education or perversion against culture. The answers suggested that people accept culture and its rules; perversion is not acceptable to culture. All cultures teach how to have sex in healthy manner; to ignore the culture's teaching leads to sexual perversion, which is often, punished or criticized.

The third question was do you enjoy sexual interaction?

All the responders seemed to enjoy sexuality. They indicated that it is a life force that creates a feeling of being alive. But two people indicated that sexuality should be just average, that an abuse of sex. It is good to fantasize, but within limits, because perversion is a bad thing. They felt people should stay within cultural limits. Some accepted sadism without elaborating how they accept it. The interviewer felt they wanted to say it was good to live out sexual fantasies. This is similar to Barthomeley's statement on sado-masochism:

> *Occasionally I am lucky enough to meet a professional dominatrice at the club preferably large, blonde, busty and clad in black leather, who is willing to put me through the process. (B.V., Spring 1998, # 52, pp. 77).*

This quote lets us know that in the mind of the lovers they share common tendencies such as sadism even if it is not acceptable to society. Human beings can be eccentric, but these practices can not be stated publicly because people know it leads to censure by society. In public people try to follow the ways of the culture. When alone with a consenting partner they indulge in practices that are quite the opposite.

K.E. from Omaha Nebraska said:

> *I love my husband, but because of my high sex drive and constant attention I get from other men, I have not been able to stay faithful to him . . . I must admit as guilty as I feel, I also feel good when I am cheating; there is also something very erotic about it. (Forum # 02217, September 1998, pp. 49).*

That quote suggests that despite her conscience she seeks to gratify her sexual urges. She wants to say that her goal is sexual gratification for which she represses her conscience. Sometimes, when some people talk about sadism publicly, they want to persuade others to indulge in similar sadistic behaviors. This may became of feeling of shame or guilt.

If their conscience condemns them, they may feel better if they are not so alone in these practices. The ideas can be contagious; if someone does not have a strong sense of values they can end up accepting the suggestion and then end up feeling shame. Talking about values Cassandra said:

> Let see . . . good little girls are quiet, withdrawn and do not say what they feel; and bad little girls (pause) say what they feel. (Sandra and Sue, 1993, pp. 166).

This suggests that sometimes people feel this can be about assertiveness.

The fifth question was: Do you believe laws can control sexuality?

The responses suggested that people like to live their sexuality without interference from law enforcement authorities. Even though they accept culture norms they would like to live their sexuality like they feel it. The interviewers felt that authorities can not control people's impulses. In the literature we see that even illegal acts are hard to control by legal authorities. This is true even of incest. Talking about his incest with his aunt, P.J. said:

> I am 17, my aunt 36 years old; She invited me during the vacation, When her husband (my uncle) was in trip, she entered in my room, pulled my sheet, insulted me . . . idiot, stupid, pig, she excited me to have sex with her. During the scene, she still insults me; after sex taking, she said: now we have a secret; does not say it to someone. (Union # 3277-149, May 1984, pp. 51).

Another reason this type of activity remains secret is that people become implicated as accomplices and become trapped with a secret. Sometimes because sexuality is spontaneous the laws can be broken and then kept secret. This can entrap the victim in illegal and unnatural and exploitative acts.

The sixth question was: Can laws control sadism and sadistic practices?

In general interviewees state that laws can't control sadism. It is hard to control vices and perversions enacted privately by consenting adults. People do not like to talk about, but they may feel comfortable enacting it.

The seventh question was: Would you like adding anything to the topic of sexuality and sadism?

Two people said nothing, two others said sexuality is life, two others said we must have good values, one said sex education must be kept private.

Briefly people think sexuality is a matter of importance in life, that it is not good to play with lightly. The interviewees all felt that it is good to have respect for sexual matters, to let people live their sexuality naturally without interference from laws.

When people finished answering to the questions, they looked very serious; but at the end of all, when I said: "thank you", they laughed! I encountered this reaction with all the interviewees. When I asked about the meaning of this they said: "You know your self ". That meant that every thing they told me I know it too, because I am human like them. Because sexuality is natural, every body has these images inside.

I think the subjects were right when they said that sexuality is natural, and that every body has the potential to perform it. People feel overtaken by natural urges and impulses. The interviewees stated that people may feel controlled by their sexual urges but it does not mean they do not have values.

CHAPTER 6

Implications of the study

Judge yourself. (Ibid. February/March 2009)

Some interviewees said: sexuality is a love, others said: it is to have sex with someone of the opposite sex. Some others said, it is to have a baby. Some people distinguished between love and sexuality. Love is a hope toward someone. In love we hope the best for a beloved, even if we do not have sex with him or her. That is a parent's love for their children, their relatives, their comrades. With these categories, when the word love is used they want to say: I hope the best things for you. In West Africa, when we say good morning to someone, we say: good morning to you, to your wife, to your kids, to your business, to your friends, to your animals. We want the best for him and his (her) environment. We want success for the beloved.

Sexuality means relations between the two sexes; these relations refer to genital sexuality. It is the responsibility of people to manage their sexuality. This includes taking responsibility for each other's physical and psychological wellbeing when engaged in sexual acts. When sexual partners think about their sexual relations, if they are responsible they care about the survival of their sexual relations. If sexuality is to have sex with someone, it is also to manage the sexual relationship, to think about the survival of the sexual relationship.

Many modern societies do not accept that the goal of sexuality is to have a baby (like some subjects said). But I believe that this is an important aspect. By sexuality, human being come into the world and enters in God's creation. Dr. George Fenerstein said about sacred sexuality for Deborah:

> *I seemed to be at the center of the cosmos, the universe opened to me.*
> *I saw the earth being created . . . (Scantling and Browder, pp. 28).*

Though it is my view that the purpose of sexuality is to procreate, people who want to have sexual pleasure often use lots of products to prevent the pregnancy.

Regarding the issue of sadism, a lot of people do not fantasize much before having sex. Sexual contact is direct and simple for them. A lot of them do not know much about sadism, and they do not practice it. However, some know sadism and practice it, but they do not like to talk about it. Often the reason is because society does not accept it, and they are ashamed to talk about it publicly.

Many people believe that sexuality is sacred. Because of this view they believe that it is good to have a positive and respectful attitude toward sexuality. In my view, it is not good to be banal about sexuality like modern civilization is doing. Sexuality is life sharing and serious business. One cannot play with it in a casual way.

Regarding fantasy. It is probably good to fantasize, but not too much, because for some people it leads to perversion and sadism which is unacceptable in my view.

To arrive at positive perspective toward healthy sexuality, lots of subjects suggested having good sex education for children and adults. Sex education needs to be organized, discreet, and presented respectfully and seriously.

Subjects of this study were clear that sexuality couldn't be blurred with sadism, which is a perversion. Sexuality is life, while sadism profits from pain, victimization and exploitation. It requires a victim masochist. Many sadists do engage in normal sex at times but this is more the exception than the rule.

During the interviews people would often smile while discussing sex. When asked they would say that talking about sex often led to visualizing it. In elaborating on this it appears that men and women fantasize about and visualize the physical aspects of the opposite sex. Women tend to focus and fantasize more about male genitalia, and men about women's genitalia. Interviewees discussed their fantasies; female subjects discussed how they could not include in their fantasies how they were going to react, because the reaction depended on the partner's actions. Interviewees by and large focussed on sex that was normal and natural. They limited discussion about different kinds of fantasies. Interviewees also state that sexuality had many manifestations and so they had difficulty in defining it.

Additional issues that arose from the literature and the interviews included themes discussed below.

A-Sexuality is imposing: When someone is living a sexual experience, it is not for free; sexuality imposes rules, and people need to play by the rules. Once involved people describe a feeling of letting go. Julia, a 34 years old school administrator said:

> I'm not thinking how I look or if I'm doing it right for me. I just am (Scantling Browder, 1993, pp. 47).

B-Sexuality is an opening: For talkative persons the period before, during or after sex they talk about their history, their life, their job, their situation. An example is Sophie, a 52 years old who said:

> During my best sexual moment, my mind is open like a hollow tube and memories and images flow through it freely, with no criticism or pressure. (Ibid, 1993, pp. 47).

Talking about sexual experience, Upanishas said:

> When before the beauty of sunset or of a mountain you pause and exclaim, Aha! You are participing in divinity. Such a moment of participation involves a realization of the wonder and sheer beauty

of existence. It is the same when by the sex you procreate, you admire the born baby; you participate in divinity creation. You are wide open to the universe. (Ibid,1993, pp. 69).

C-Sexuality is feeling connection: Drs Scantling and Browder, citing psychoanalyst Eric Fromm, wrote:

"the human desire to experience union with others is one of the strongest motivators of human behavior". (Ibid, 1993, pp. 110).

Good manner. (Ibid. February/March 2009)

Many say: sex is a unifier, it puts together two people; this unity can ignite a big unity for two families, two villages, two countries or even the world. That is why some subjects said they were in the center of the Universe. Some subjects said that laws cannot control sexuality. They felt that sexuality is primal and only nature can control it. It is transcultural and transcendent, governed by the principles that govern the universe. In their book, Scantling and Browder noted:

the women transcend many cultural messages about what we "should" think, feel, and do to have intensely an erotic experience. Among these are some myths. That the best way to enliven one's sex life is to focus on changing some thing. (Ibid, 1993, pp.16).

D-Sexuality is sacred: George F. finds that the kind of sexual experience lived by Deborah is a sign of sacred sexuality. She felt she was participating via that experience in divine creation. Sexuality was viewed as nature, not governable by human laws.

E-Sexuality is sharing: the subjects both male and female put into the sexual encounter the best of themselves and gave to their partner all they could give and do. If a child is conceived many described how they looked for aspects of both parents: this part comes from father, that one comes from mather. Like Scantling and Browder said:

> *These women express the conviction that each sexual experience is to be enjoyed purely for what it has to offer. (Ibid, 1993, pp. 51).*

Sexuality can be a difficult problem because one is expecting to give oneself as a gift to another who is going to do the same. This involves generosity. Two people have the same problem, same difficulty, same sharing idea, same gift of the body and mind. That is why many hesitate became it is a serious act.

F-Sexuality is a problem: In my view it is gift human beings received from God upon creation. It is the beginning of our life. We have to nurture it and develop it by good education for life; sexuality by education has to be used without disturbing other body functions. Education can help to avoid the confusion between the body parts. Authors Scantling and Browder underlined:

> *There are the most important qualities a woman must develop before she can reach supersexual bliss. Why? Because our excitation of what's possible, limits our capacities. To become supersexual, a woman may have to transcend many of the ways she has been culturally trained to think of sex. The more vividly you are able to imagine this, the more pleasurable the feeling can become. pp. 104).*

And Shakespeare said:

> *We are such stuff as dreams are made of. What we imagine and how we imagine affects our conscious realty. (pp. 201).*

That means again that there are no limits in imagination or feelings. Some people's imagination can go to sadism. Imagination is good, but not beyond acceptable limits.

But we have Sadism: In my view, people confuse sexuality and sexual sadism because this sadism occurs when the people want to have or are having intercourse; sadists profit from sexuality that inflicts pain on the consenting partner when having sex. As a fantasy, it can be considered to be a perversion which is not acceptable by society. The perverts try to contaminate lots of people to accept it; but many societies do not accept it.

Sadism is closely linked to power and domination with one person having to submit. Since all cultures focus on sexual practices being enacted in an acceptable manner, sadism continues without talking about it publicly. Parents have a mission to educate children to know about healthy sexual relations and to avoid the unhealthy ones. If children don't receive a good sexual education, they could fall prey to unsavory experiences or per

Bad manner by writing on the body. (Ibid. February/March 2009)

Sexuality is not sadism and sadism is not sexuality. Sexuality is life force; sadism is a force of despair and pain. There is no way the two are interchangeable.

It was my hope, in this paper, to explore the differences and the continuum between sexuality and sadism.

BIBLIOGRAPHY

Chaplin, J.P.: Dictionary of Psychology 1985. Second revised edition: edition: Laurel.

Gray, John.: Men are from Mars, women are from Venus, 1951, edition: The library of congress cataloging-in-publication.

Forum September 1998, edition: A Penthouse Publication

Forum. February 1998, edition: A Penthouse publication.

Scantling, S. and S. Browder: Ordinary Women, Extraordinary Sex 1993,

Edition: Library of Congress Cataloging in Publication Data.

Sharf, Richard: Theory of Psychology and Counseling: Concepts and Cases

1999, edition: Library of Congress Cataloging in Publication Data.

Time Magazine. March 15, 1999, edition Times

Union 33277-149, November 1984, edition: Union

Union, Special series Union: edition Union.

Variation. Spring, 1998, edition: Association publisher.